# Dividend Stock Investing
For People Who Have No Clue Where to Start

Bryan Kelley

Self-Published with Kindle Direct Publishing

Copyright © 2022 by Bryan K. Kelley

ISBN: 9798827561378

All rights reserved. No part of this publication may be reproduced, distributed, or transmitted in any form or by any means, including photocopying, recording, or other electronic or mechanical methods, without the prior written permission of the publisher, except in the case of brief quotations embodied in critical reviews and certain other noncommercial uses permitted by copyright law. For permission requests, write to the publisher, addressed "Attention: Permissions Coordinator," at the email address below.

Kindle Direct Publishing
Amazon.com Services LLC,
410 Terry Ave N
Seattle, WA 98109

Ordering Information:
Amazon.com

Printed in the United States of America

For Permission Contact:
curious.kelley.travel.blog@gmail.com

**Dedicated to my amazing siblings...**

Jenny Bentley

Sarah Keaton

Seth Kelley

Jesse Kelley

Felisha Matthews

Melissa Daniel

In any moment of decision, the best thing you can do is the right thing, the next best thing is the wrong thing, and the worst thing you can do is nothing.

**Theodore Roosevelt**

## Disclaimer:

The risk of investing in certain financial instruments, including those mentioned in this book, is generally high, as their market value is exposed to a lot of different factors such as the operational and financial conditions of the relevant company, country of economy, growth prospects, change in interest rates, the economic and political environment, foreign exchange rates, shifts in market sentiments, etc. Where an investment or security is denominated in a different currency to the investor's currency of reference, change in rates of exchange may have an adverse effect on the value, price or income or from that investment to the investor. Investors investing in funds denominated in non-local currency should be aware of the risk of exchange rate fluctuations that may cause a loss of principal. Any past performance, projection, forecast or simulation of results is not necessarily indicative of the future or likely performance of any investment. Estimates of future performance are based on assumptions that may not be realized. Potential for profit is accompanied by the possibility of loss. The value of investments and the income from them may go down as well as go up. When investing in individual instruments or financial products, the investor may lose all or part of the investments. Assets allocation, diversification and rebalancing strategies do not ensure gains nor guarantee against loss. The use of leverage, shorting, and derivative strategies may accelerate the velocity of the potential losses. The use of currency strategies involves additional risks.

# Contents

**Volume 2:** .................................................................................................7
**Background and education:** ..............................................................8
**Considerations:** ...............................................................................11
**Planning your investment strategy:** ................................................13
**Review your timeframe and risk tolerance:** ....................................15
**Seeking help from a professional:** ..................................................18
**Consider where to invest your money:** ..........................................20
**Basic Logic and Reasoning:** .............................................................23
**The Down & Dirty on Diversification:** .............................................30
    Investing in stock sectors ..............................................................31
        1. Energy Sector ......................................................................32
        2. Materials Sector ..................................................................33
        3. Industrials Sector ................................................................34
        4. Utilities Sector ....................................................................35
        5. Healthcare Sector ...............................................................36
        6. Financials Sector .................................................................37
        7. Consumer Discretionary Sector .........................................38
        8. Consumer Staples Sector ....................................................39
        9. Information Technology Sector .........................................40
        10. Communication Services Sector ......................................41
        11. Real Estate Sector .............................................................42
**Stocks to Buy:** .................................................................................45
    Stocks at around $50.00 – ..............................................................47
    Stocks around $85.00 - ..................................................................49
    Stocks around $150.00 – ...............................................................50
**Where can you buy stocks?** ............................................................52
**Retirement and Dividends:** .............................................................54
**Conclusion:** .....................................................................................59

## Volume 2:

This book will be the second book in this series of dividend investing books. Each book will have three new recommendations accompanied with an explanation of why I would recommend those particular three dividend stocks. For those of you that don't want to have to do any research or homework, I will hand you three solid choices.

Each book will follow the same format as all the other books in the series, so it won't matter which book you pick to start with or end with. They will all keep it simple and explain things in a way that should be easy for just about anyone to follow along and understand.

Whether you buy just one, or buy the whole series, you will learn something and walk away with some solid choices for some dividend stocks that you can add to your portfolio or to start your portfolio with.

## Background and education:

Here is the straight scoop. I'm just a blue-collar guy with no formal financial education. I did go to college for business and I have started, built, managed and sold a few different businesses, but none of those had anything to do with the financial management industry.

The information I will be sharing with you all comes from the school of hard knocks, not from Harvard. It will be completely up to you to consider anything I mention in this book very carefully. I will be sharing what will be considered grade school level financial information (at best) compared to what other more formally educated people might offer. But basic and simple is the whole idea behind my books. If you already knew how to do it, or what to do, then you certainly wouldn't be reading anything of mine.

I won't be using a lot of the terms and jargon that others might use, and that is by design. As I mentioned, I am going for simple.

I have dealt with the public most of my professional career. One thing has remained true more times than not. People just want to be handed an answer.

When I sold tires, customers rarely wanted to hear all the technical stuff I could go on and on about. They rarely wanted all that technical jargon and probably didn't understand much of it when I offered it to them. What they wanted was to be told what to get, by the person in front of them selling it. And they relied on my suggestions and personal experience to help them make a good choice. If they didn't like the price, they wanted another good option to consider in their price point. It was just that simple

That is basically the goal of these books. To offer my experiences without boring you with all the jargon you probably don't care to hear or don't want to try and understand anyway. You just want some good options, with some quick and easy information that you can easily understand.

If it makes sense, appeals to your situation, and you think it works for you, then you might consider it. If you don't, at least you have the information to reference later.

Straight forward, to the point and simple. In the Marine core we called it the K.I.S.S principle. K.I.S.S stands for Keep It Simple Stupid. There is no reason to over complicate things when you can just keep it simple.

**THE KISS PRINCIPLE | KEEP IT SIMPLE, STUPID**

## Considerations:

What exactly does a person need to start any kind of investing? The most obvious answer of course is money. It seems like a no brainer, but I am going to talk about it just a little bit to fill you in on a few things that you may not have thought about.

The first thing to consider is... what is your goal? What do you want this money to do for you? Most people that are considering investing want their money to make them more money. This is similar to the concept of a bank that pays you interest. You keep your money at the bank, and the bank in turn pays you a very minuscule amount to keep it there.

The second thing to consider is how much can you afford? This is different for everyone of course, but you will benefit from sitting down and itemizing everything on a piece of paper or a spreadsheet so you can visualize your own situation. Once you have everything itemized, you can start to calculate an amount that is realistic for you to invest.

The last thing to consider is your timeframe. How long are you going to give yourself to reach your goals. Or for some of you, it might be, how much longer do you have to try and reach your goals. When considering your time frame, you should also consider how much risk you are willing to take on.

As an example, I am 50 years old while I am writing this. I have to ask myself...

- How much longer do I want to work?
- How much longer will I be physically able to work?
- What age do I want to retire at?

## Planning your investment strategy:

One of the main things to consider before investing is having some sort of plan. Have you ever heard the saying, "If you aim at nothing, you will hit is every time?" That definitely applies here in a big way. By formulating some sort of plan, it will help you put into perspective not only your investment goals, but when and how you want to achieve them. It can also help to remove the likelihood of emotions influencing your investment decisions.

There's no denying that the nature of investing can be emotional. I have heard many successful investors over and over again say, "make a plan and stick with it." There will be times where you may feel tempted to change your investment strategy because an area of your portfolio is not doing well, or you received recent news the market is going to plummet, or you get some "hot tip."

While these events may cause you to react quickly, such as selling off your positions, it's important to stop and take a moment to consider your investment strategy. If your approach is intended to be a long-term plan, making decisions based on short-term market fluctuations, may greatly affect what you set out to achieve.

You will certainly benefit more from removing as much of the emotions out of it as possible, and just sticking to the plan you made. This of course does not in any way mean that you can't revise your plan as you grow and learn better information. The point I am trying to drive home here is, be smart, not emotional.

## Review your timeframe and risk tolerance:

As I mentioned earlier, it's important to consider how much time you're giving yourself to build towards your financial goal and how much risk you're prepared to take on to get there.

For example, an investment plan for retirement may look very different to someone who is much older or younger. If you're looking to access your money in a shorter time frame, remaining invested through ups and downs in the market may be unlikely, so a less risky investment approach may work to your favor.

Now I am going to pretty much only cover blue chip stocks which typically are very low risk. But there are never any guarantees so you always have to consider and investments as a risk.

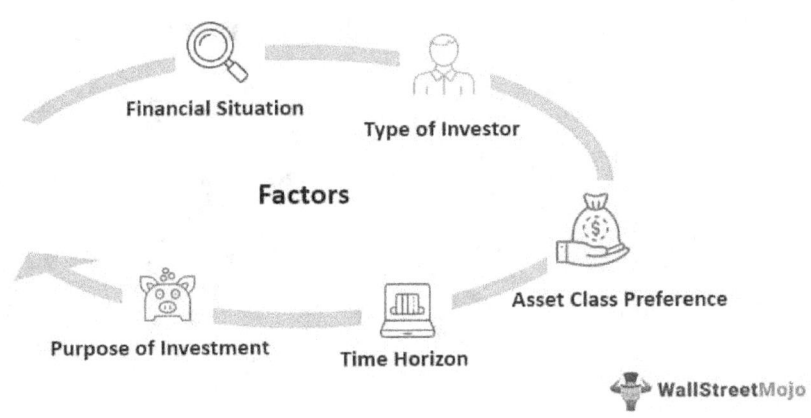

I'll give you a personal case that happened to me with one of my investments. I chose AT&T as one stock that would be a good safe bet. This is a company that has been around for almost 40 years. They have over $168 billion in revenue. They have very consistently raised their dividends year after year. And since that is about as much criteria as I need for my basic research, that was good enough for me.

Recently, AT&T stock Fell as the company announced a WarnerMedia Spin-Off and cut its dividends. Without going too much into the technical stuff, shares of AT&T gained downside momentum after the company announced that it would spin off its interest in WarnerMedia to shareholders at closing of the merger with Discovery. Because the market is emotional, share prices dropped and the company decreased its dividend.

This is how that affected me. First, my stock value dropped from where I was buying a single share at around $26.00, to now you can buy them at around $20.00. That means I lost around $6.00 of value per share that I owned. In addition, my quarterly dividend dropped from $0.52 per share down to $0.278 per share.

As you can see from that example, there is always risk. A Great company, with great history, longevity and revenue. And still it was not immune to problems that can arise for any company at any time. So always keep in mind that there is risk.

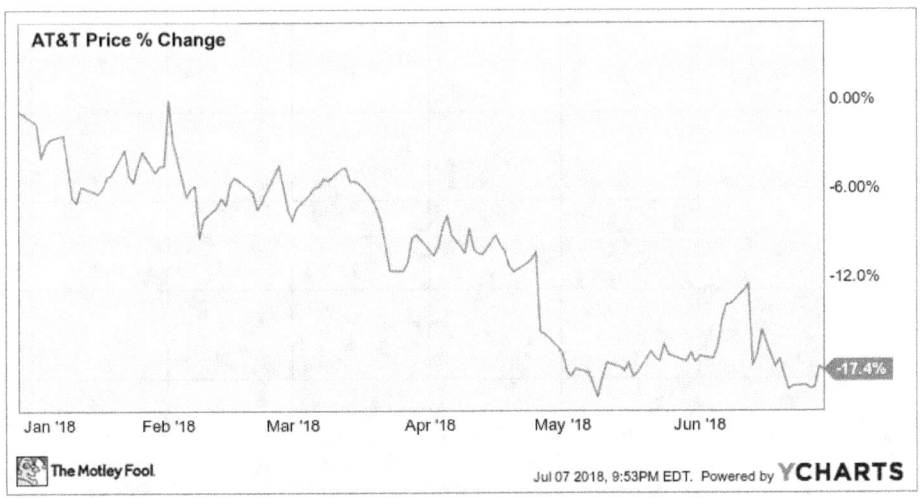

## Seeking help from a professional:

If you value the experience of experts in other aspects of your life, don't discount it when it comes to managing your life savings or investing.

A financial adviser is not just someone who helps with investments. Their job is to help you with every aspect of your financial life—savings, insurance, tax, debt—while keeping you on track to achieve your goals.

More importantly, they can answer questions like:

- What age can I stop working and retire?
- What strategies can I use to build my wealth?
- How can I ensure my wealth is transferred to my children?

If your to-do list is endless and you never quite have time to tackle your personal finances, a financial adviser may help to set you on the right track. They are certainly worth considering, but I don't suggest just going to anyone that isn't recommended by someone else.

Picking a financial advisor or someone to manage your investments is also not without risk. Not only are they dealing with the same market everyone else is in, they get paid fees for helping you. My brother just picked a random company and person and ended up paying more in fees than he made with the investments. So be careful when considering a professional because there are bad ones out there.

## Consider where to invest your money:

You may choose to divvy up your money across a variety of positions (stocks). And this is something I would highly recommend doing. Try not to "put all your eggs in one basket." When we talk about risk, having all your eggs in one basket is just far too risky.

Diversification - One of the main advantages of investing in different positions (stocks), is the ability to diversify your risk. This means, if one of your investments doesn't perform well, your losses may not be as significant as if you only invest in the one asset class, as your other investments may help to level it out. I'll touch more on this later.

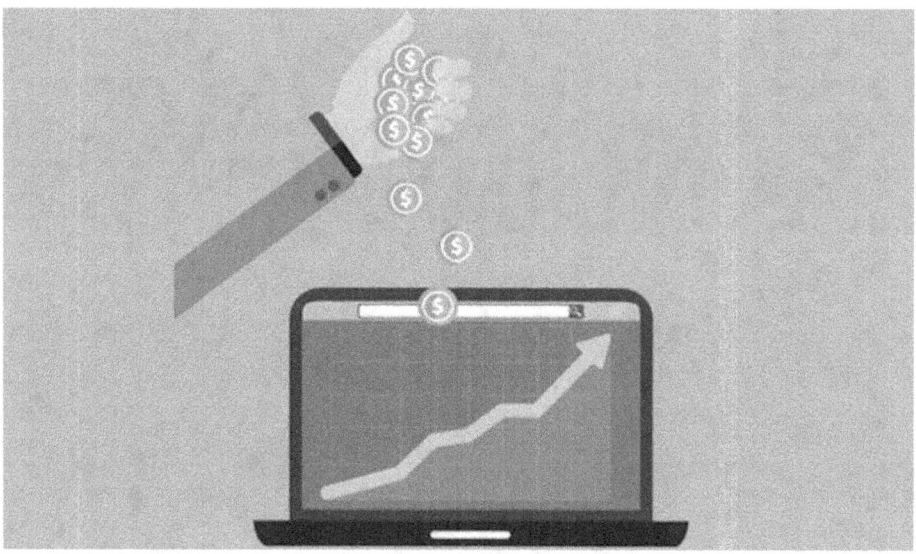

Consider the company not just share price - If you're investing in shares, it's also important to look beyond the stock price, the dividend, and consider the company you're buying into. If it's values and goals don't sit well with you, then it may not be the best investment option for you.

Most people don't have to look to far to find what they are interested in and it doesn't take anyone to long to remember things they don't like. Just apply that to considering buying dividend stocks. Remember, it doesn't have to be complicated.

There are plenty of great companies we engage with on a regular basis. In fact, a typical working day might involve consuming the products and services of literally dozens of publicly-traded companies.

For instance, we might wake up in the morning to the sound of our iPhone's alarm. We'll drive to work in his beloved **Ford** (NYSE:F) F150. On the way, we might stop for a skinny latte at **Starbucks** (NYSE:SBUX), which we will pay for with our **MasterCard** (NYSE:MA). At work, we'll power up our desktop and open a Windows Excel spreadsheet.

In just one morning, we have made use of multiple different companies: **Apple** (NASDAQ:AAPL), Ford, Starbucks, MasterCard, **Microsoft** (NASDAQ:MSFT), **Atlassian** (NASDAQ:TEAM), and **Facebook** (NASDAQ:FB).

Of these companies, the one we might decide that we love best is the one whose core product we use at the beginning and the end of each day — Apple. So that is what we end up choosing.

## Basic Logic and Reasoning:

My Basic Criteria for Choosing Dividend Stocks:

I'll cover some of my basic criteria for choosing the dividend stocks that I purchase.

First and foremost, it has to be considered a "blue-chip" stock. What exactly is a blue-chip stock? Simply put, a blue chip is a nationally recognized, well-established, and financially sound company. Blue chips generally sell high-quality, widely accepted products and services. Blue-chip companies are known to weather downturns and operate profitably in the face of adverse economic conditions, which helps to contribute to their long record of stable and reliable growth.

Off the top of your head, what are a few recognizable brands that you can think of? Did you think of companies like Coca-Cola, Disney, PepsiCo, Walmart, General Electric, IBM, and McDonald's? If you did, you would be correct because these are all dominant leaders in their respective industries. Blue-chip companies like these have built a reputable brand over the years and the fact that they have survived multiple downturns in the economy makes them stable companies to have in a portfolio.

Second, I want it to pay a good dividend.

What is a stock dividend? A stock dividend is a dividend payment to shareholders that is made in shares rather than as cash. The stock dividend has the advantage of rewarding shareholders without reducing the company's cash balance, although it should be noted, and shareholders should be aware that companies can dilute earnings per share.

Why is investing in dividend stocks a good idea? Dividend-paying stocks provide a way for investors to get paid during rocky market periods, when capital gains are hard to achieve. They provide a nice hedge against inflation, especially when they grow over time. They are tax advantaged, unlike other forms of income, such as interest on fixed-income investments.

What is an easy way to find out what a company or a stock pays out in dividends? I use the internet. Just about everyone has a cell phone or a computer these days, so finding out this information is easy. You can just type in McDonald's stock dividend. Scroll down and select whichever site you want and you will find that as of today's date (5/8/22) that they pay $1.38 per share quarterly. The current share price is $250.78, so getting paid $1.38 on that amount is way better than what a bank will pay you. And as a bonus, if you had purchased the stock back in 2018 when share prices were $178, then you would have also gained all that additional stock or share value.

Do some quick math... That is over $70 you gained in value per share plus the dividends which would have been around $20 total. In this example you made roughly $90 per share over 4 years. I challenge you to find any bank that would have paid anything even close to that.

Now one site that I like to look at and use most when finding information about stock dividends is the www.nasdaq.com site. You can look at whichever site tickles your fancy, but I like this one because it is super easy to read. There is nothing to figure out and the information is all right there easy and accessible. I just type in *"McDonalds stock dividend"* or I use the ticker symbol MCD to search the internet. Then when the options pop us, I scroll down to the Nasdaq site, click on it and check it out.

As you can plainly see in this illustration, McDonald's currently pays a quarterly dividend of $1.38 per share. You can also easily see the history of what they have paid each quarter. And in this case, you can easily see that McDonald's has steadily, and regularly increased their dividend over time.

Now in my opinion, this is as complicated as I get. This is obviously a great stock to own not only because the stock price or value has steadily risen, but they have also steadily increased the dividend. And I think it is pretty safe to say that McDonald's as a company isn't going under any time soon.

At this point, there are really only a few details to answer before you consider buying a stock like this. Do you want to support the fast food industry and McDonald's as a company (which I cover briefly down below)? And do you want to pay (at the time of this writing) $245.04 per share (which I also briefly cover down below)?

Third, do I like the company or want to invest in it? Besides making money, what are some other things to consider? Things like business practices, do my values align with the company values and practices. One example might be... If you don't drink alcohol, do you choose to invest in an alcohol company?

For me personally, I don't care for Nike. I prefer Under Armour because I am a Veteran and Under Armour supports The Wounded Warrior Project. For those of you who are not familiar, The Wounded Warrior Project is a legitimate multimillion-dollar nonprofit organization with nationwide recognition that helps wounded, ill and injured veterans. So for personal reason, I choose to invest in Under Armour regardless of any possibility that Nike might be more profitable.

Fourth is price range. What exactly can I afford? How much bang do I get for my buck? McDonald's is a great stock to buy, but it is around $250 a share. Right now, I could buy Verizon for $48 a share and get a $0.64 dividend per share per quarter. That means I could buy five shares of Verizon for the price of one share of McDonald's. And I would have a total of $3.20 per share in dividends per quarter. But Verizon's stock value has not done near what McDonald's has. As a matter of fact, depending on where you bought Verizon in 2018, you may have lost a few dollars of value.

## The Down & Dirty on Diversification:

I touched on this earlier, but this is worth just a little more explanation so when you go to make some choices, you can make some good ones.

Sector: A stock market sector is a group of stocks that have a lot in common with each other, usually because they are in similar industries. There are 11 different stock market sectors, according to the most commonly used classification system: the Global Industry Classification Standard (GICS).

Stocks are categorized into sectors to make it easy to compare companies that have similar business models. When investing, you can choose from stocks within the sectors that interest you. Sectors also make it easier to compare which stocks are making the most money. This helps you make decisions about what your next investments will be.

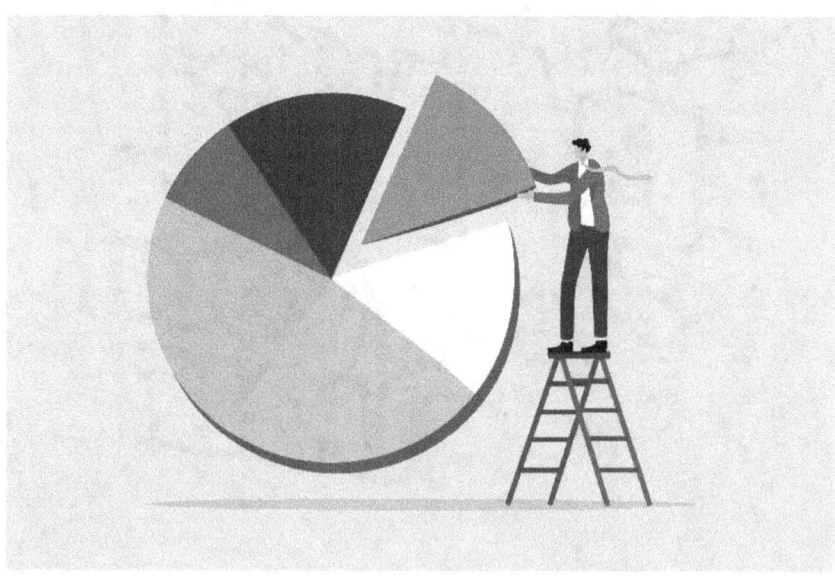

# Investing in stock sectors

At a glance, the 11 GICS stock market sectors are...

1. Energy
2. Materials
3. Industrials
4. Utilities
5. Healthcare
6. Financials
7. Consumer Discretionary
8. Consumer Staples
9. Information Technology
10. Communication Services
11. Real Estate

## 1. Energy Sector

The energy sector covers companies that do business in the oil and natural gas industry. It includes oil and gas exploration and production companies, as well as producers of other consumable fuels like coal and ethanol. The energy sector also includes the related businesses that provide equipment, materials, and services to oil and gas producers. Oddly enough, though, it doesn't include many renewable energy companies, which instead are considered utilities.

The largest U.S. stocks in the energy sector are **ExxonMobil** ([NYSE:XOM](NYSE:XOM)) and **Chevron** ([NYSE:CVX](NYSE:CVX)).

## 2. Materials Sector

The materials sector includes companies that provide various goods for use in manufacturing and other applications. You'll find makers of chemicals, construction materials, and containers and packaging within the materials sector, along with mining stocks and companies specializing in making paper and forest products.

Well-known materials stocks include paint maker **Sherwin-Williams** (NYSE:SHW) and chemicals manufacturer **DuPont** (NYSE:DD).

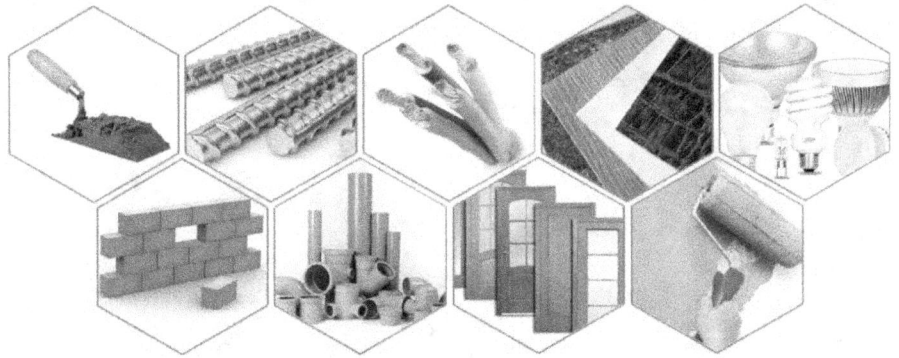

## 3. Industrials Sector

The industrials sector encompasses a wide range of different businesses that generally involve the use of heavy equipment. Transportation stocks such as airlines, railroads, and logistics companies are found within the industrials sector, as are companies in the aerospace, defense, construction, and engineering industries. Companies making building products, electrical equipment, and machinery also fall into this sector, as do many conglomerates.

**Boeing** (NYSE:BA) and **Union Pacific** (NYSE:UNP) are among the largest U.S. industrials stocks.

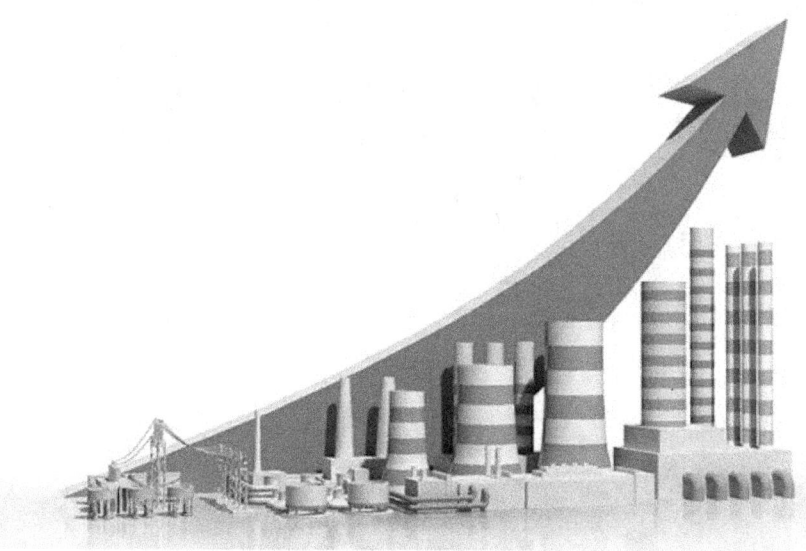

## 4. Utilities Sector

The utilities sector encompasses just about every different type of utility company you can think of. Within the sector, you'll find utilities specializing in making electrical power available to residential and commercial customers, as well as specialists in natural gas transmission and distribution. Other utilities are responsible for delivering water to customers. Some utility companies engage in more than one of these different subspecialties. In addition, independent producers of power and renewable electricity also land in the utilities sector, even though they don't exactly resemble the traditional regulated utility in an era of deregulation.

Utilities tend to be regional in scope, so you might have heard of **Duke Energy** (NYSE:DUK) in the Southeast U.S., **Consolidated Edison** (NYSE:ED) in the Northeast, and **American Electric Power** (NASDAQ:AEP) across much of the Ohio Valley and the Southern Plains states.

## 5. Healthcare Sector

The healthcare sector has two primary components. One component includes companies that develop pharmaceuticals and treatments based on biotechnology, as well as the analytical tools and supplies needed for the clinical trials that test those treatments. The other encompasses healthcare equipment and services, including surgical supplies, medical diagnostic tools, and health insurance.

**UnitedHealth Group** (NYSE:UNH) and **Johnson & Johnson** (NYSE:JNJ) are the two stocks at the top of the healthcare sector.

## 6. Financials Sector

The financials sector includes businesses that are primarily related to handling money. Banks are a key industry group within the sector, but you'll also find insurance companies, brokerage houses, consumer finance providers, and mortgage-related real estate investment trusts among financials.

Warren Buffett's **Berkshire Hathaway** (NYSE:BRK-A) (NYSE:BRK-B) and financial giant **JPMorgan Chase** (NYSE:JPM) are among the best-known stocks in the financials sector.

## 7. Consumer Discretionary Sector

The consumer discretionary sector covers goods and services for which consumer demand depends upon consumer financial status. For example, if you make $25,000 per year, you probably buy a different car than someone who makes $25 million per year. The sector includes companies that sell higher-priced items like automobiles and luxury goods, as well as leisure products. You'll find both brick-and-mortar and e-commerce-based retail companies in this category, along with hotel and restaurant stocks.

**Amazon.com** (NASDAQ:AMZN) and **McDonald's** (NYSE:MCD) are among the biggest stocks in the sector.

## 8. Consumer Staples Sector

The consumer staples sector includes goods and services that consumers need, regardless of their current financial condition. The category includes companies in the food, beverage, and tobacco industries, as well as household and personal care products. You'll also find retail companies that specialize in selling staples, such as supermarkets, in this group.

**Coca-Cola** (NYSE:KO) and **Procter & Gamble** (NYSE:PG) are two of the most valuable consumer staples stocks in the U.S. market.

## 9. Information Technology Sector

The information technology sector covers companies involved in the different categories of technological innovation. Some companies in information technology focus on creating software or providing services related to implementing technological solutions, while others are more involved in building the equipment, components, and hardware that make tech possible. Information technology also includes makers of semiconductors and the" equipment used to produce semiconductor chips.

**Apple** (NASDAQ:AAPL) and **Microsoft** (NASDAQ:MSFT) have been switching places back and forth at the top of the list of large U.S. stocks in the information technology sector.

## 10. Communication Services Sector

The communication services sector is the newest of the GICS sectors and includes a couple of major areas that used to be part of other sectors. Telecommunication services providers, including both wireless telecom networks and providers of old-style landline services, make up one wing of the sector. At the other end are media and entertainment companies, including both older media like television and radio and interactive media via the internet and newer forms of communication.

Social media giant **Facebook** (NASDAQ:FB) and search engine pioneer **Alphabet** (NASDAQ:GOOGL) (NASDAQ:GOOG) are among the biggest stocks in communication services.

## 11. Real Estate Sector

The real estate sector generally includes two different types of investments related to real estate. Some stocks in the sector are responsible for developing new real estate projects and then managing them by obtaining tenants for various spaces within the project property. In addition, most real estate investment trusts, which are special tax-favored business entities that operate in various areas of the real estate industry, get counted as within the real estate sector.

Among the top stocks in the real estate sector, you'll find cellular communications tower specialist **American Tower** (NYSE:AMT) and major shopping mall owner and operator **Simon Property Group** (NYSE:SPG).

Industry:

Industry vs. Sector - An Overview

Although they may seem the same, the terms industry and sector have slightly different meanings. Industry refers to a much more specific group of companies or businesses, while the term sector describes a large segment of the economy.

The terms industry and sector are often used interchangeably to describe a group of companies that operate in the same segment of the economy or share a similar business type. The term sector often refers to a larger, general part of the economy, while the word industry is much more specific.

These two terms are sometimes reversed. But the general idea remains: one breaks the economy down into a few general segments while the other further categorizes those into more specific business activities. In the stock market, the generally accepted terminology cites a sector as a broad classification and an industry as a more specific one.

Having a little understanding of these terms is important so you don't put all your eggs in one basket like I talked about earlier. Part of diversifying your portfolio is making sure that you buy some of each. As I mentioned, you want to try and create a risk management strategy that mixes a wide variety of investments within your portfolio. This means, buy some Apple Stock, then buy some Exxon Mobil stock, then buy some US Bank stock. They are all stocks, but each company deals in different things. In this case, if you had these three stocks, you would have a diversified portfolio that contained a mix of distinct asset types in an attempt to limit your exposure to and single asset or risk.

## Stocks to Buy:

Now that we have covered some extremely basic information, let's move onto what most people really want to know. What stocks do I buy and why?

First and foremost, my first recommendation is... when you buy a stock, buy what you want to keep for at least 10 years. Trust me when I tell you, statistically speaking, this is the best plan to implement and here is why I am recommending the 10-year rule.

According to Ibbotson's Yearbook, over a 10-year holding period, stocks outperform any other asset class 83% of the time. If you look at a 20-year holding period, stocks outperform 98.5% of the time. However, when you get down to a five-year holding period, stocks only outperform 77% of the time, and for a one-year period stocks outperform 63% of the time.

As you can see with those stats, it would appear that 10 years should be an acceptable timeframe that should allow you to achieve the growth you are after.

With that in mind, I'm going to make some recommendations for you to consider and I will give you the basic logic and reasoning why I would recommend them. You can weigh in on it and decide as you see fit.

## Stocks at around $50.00 –
*Cardinal Health Inc (CAH).*

This stock is in the Healthcare Sector and is in the pharmaceutical industry. If you go online and type in Cardinal Health, or use the ticker symbol and type CAHFE stock, scroll down to the graph and on the "max" timeline option on the graph you can see the history dating all the way back to 1983.

The fact that the history goes back to 1983 tells you this is a long-standing business which is something we are looking for. Run your cursor over the graph at the 2012 date and you will see that 10 years ago the stock price was around $42.00. And today, the stock price is around $56.00. So sticking with the 10 year rule just potentially made us $14.00 per share. Now go to Nasdaq.com and you can see that dating all the way back to 2013, they have steadily and consistently raised their stock dividend and today you are earning $0.496 per share per quarter.

That means that your $56.00 could potentially earn you $34.00 in the next 10 years. Now we all no there isn't a bank out there that will pay that in interest. Is there? Spoiler alert! It isn't going to happen. But you can invest in dividend stocks and do quite well.

It is just that easy folks. From my perspective after listening to countless hours of financial "experts" and successful investors on YouTube, reading books and attending seminars, this is what it boils down to. There really is no big secret to picking stocks. It really and truly can be just that easy.

Stocks around $85.00 -
*Archer Daniels Midland Co. (ADM).*

This stock is in the Consumer Staples Sector and is in food processing industry. Same song second verse... If you go online and type in Archer Daniels Midland stock, or use the ticker symbol and type ADM stock, scroll down to the graph and on the "max" timeline option on the graph you can see the history dating all the way back to 1982.

Again, the long history is favorable and to some degree shows us that this is a long-standing stable company. Now run your cursor over the graph back to 2012 and you will see that the stock price back then was around $30.00. Today's price is around $85.00 so that means our 10-year rule just made around $55.00 per share. Now go to Nasdaq.com and you can see that dating all the way back to 2013, they have steadily and consistently raised their stock dividend and today you are earning $0.40 per share per quarter.

Stocks around $150.00 –

*Apple Inc (AAPL)*

This stock is in the Information Technology sector and in the consumer electronics industry. Go online and type in Apple stock, or type in the ticker symbol AAPL stock, scroll down to the graph on the "max" timeline option on the graph you can see this company dates all the way back to 1976.

Another long-standing company that would be good to consider having in a portfolio. Move your cursor to 2012 and you will see that the stock prices were around $18.00. If you would have invested back then you would have made a killing because today those stock prices are around $147.00. Just like in the examples above, let's go check out Nasdaq.com and you will see that dating back to 2013, this company has steadily increased their stock dividends and today you are earning $0.23 per share per quarter.

This one is a bit unique because Apple has split it's shares a few times. So don't get confused or worried when you see on the Nasdaq chart that the dividend went down.

Apple's stock has split five times since the company went public. The stock split on a 4-for-1 basis on August 28, 2020, a 7-for-1 basis on June 9, 2014, and split on a 2-for-1 basis on February 28, 2005, June 21, 2000, and June 16, 1987.

Companies typically engage in a stock split so that investors can more easily buy and sell shares, otherwise known as increasing the company's liquidity. Stock splits divide a company's shares into more shares, which in turn lowers a share's price and increases the number of shares available.

## How a Stock Split Works: 4-for-1 Split Example

1 Apple Share
$200

1 Apple Share
$50

1 Apple Share
$50

1 Apple Share
$50

1 Apple Share
$50

## Where can you buy stocks?

Now that I have shared a few different stocks for you to consider adding to your portfolio, how do you go about doing that? How does someone buy stocks?

In today's world, it has become very easy. You can choose to buy or sell stock on your own by opening a brokerage account with one of the many brokerage firms. After opening your account, connect it with your bank checking account to make deposits, which are then available for you to invest in.

Here are a few of the online brokers that are available...

- Charles Schwab.
- Fidelity Investments.
- TD Ameritrade.
- Robinhood.
- E-Trade.
- Interactive Brokers.
- Merrill Edge.

I'm not going to say that anyone company is any better than the other, but the one my family and I choose to use is Robinhood. All of your purchases are free, meaning there is no fee to purchase any stocks besides what you are paying for the stock itself. When you sell stocks, there is a small fee based on the dollar volume of stock you sell. It is some small fee like $0.05 to $0.10 per $1,000.00. So the fees are pretty small.

And if anyone reading this wants to join, then use my link and we will each get a free stock join.robinhood.com/bryank481. This is one of the perks of using Robinhood is that you can sign up, and once you do, you can share your link with friends. If one of those friends signs up, then you both get a free stock as a reward.

You can easily download the Robinhood app onto your phone which makes it very easy to access any time you like.

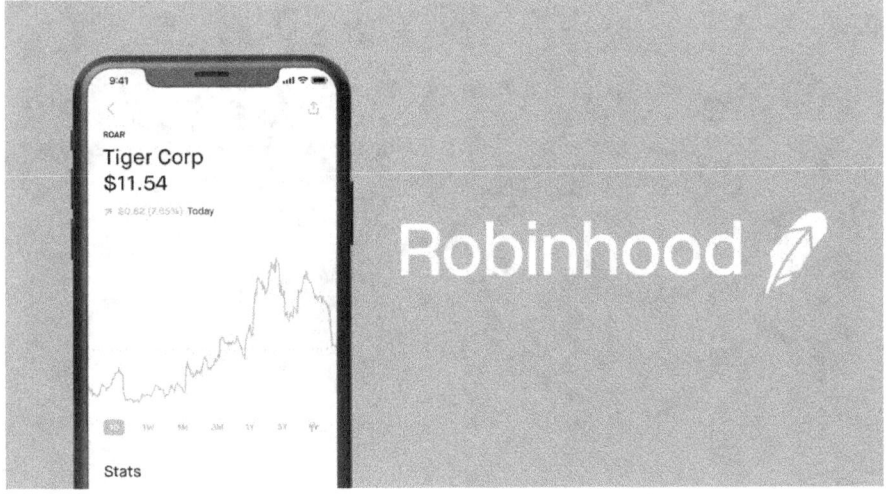

## Retirement and Dividends:

This is a bit of a crazy question that is not simple to answer because first you have to figure out how much you think you are going to need to live on at the age you retire.

Let's just do some very simple math for the sake of argument. Let's say you will need to live on $100k per year when you retire. At a 5% interest rate that would be a 2-million-dollar nest egg.

Let's say for the fun of it that you want to live off your stock dividends when you retire. Well, $100k per year is $8,334 per month. Let's make this really simple and just buy one stock all at once.

One recommendation I made in volume 1 was a monthly dividend stock. Realty Income Corp (O) was $70 a share at that time and paid a monthly dividend of $0.247.

So if you were to by all of this stock at once at $70 per share, you would have to buy 34,000 shares for the cost of $2,380,000 which would pay $8,398 per month.

Now this quick illustration does not take into account all the variables like stock price increases, etc. But this illustration should help bring across a very good point which is... Don't waste any more time! Get to work on investing as early on as you can so you increase the likelihood that you will be able to achieve whatever financial goals you are setting for yourself.

## Dividend Stocks to Research:

**Monthly Dividend Stocks –**

Ellington Financial (EFC)

Dynex Capital (DX)

Broadmark Realty Capital (BRMK)

Horizon Technology Finance (HRZN)

Shaw Communications (SJR)

LTC Properties (LTC)

PennantPark Floating Rate (PFLT)

Oxford Lane Capital (OXLC)

Cornerstone Total Return Fund (CRF)

Cornerstone Strategic Value Fund (CLM)

Pembina (PBA)

Stag Industrial STAG

Main Street Capital (MAIN)

EPR Properties (EPR)

Stellus Capital Investment Corp (SCM)

**Quarterly Dividend Stocks –**

Ares Capital (ARCC)

Verizon (VZ)

STORE Capital (STOR)

First Energy (FE)

Huntington Bank (HBAN)

Medical Properties Trust (MPW)

William Cos. (WMB)

Marathon Petroleum (MPC)

Citizens Bank (CFG)

Exxon Mobile (XOM)

People's United Bank (PBCT)

Franklin Resources (BEN)

Leggett & Platt (LEG)

Walgreens (WBA)

H&R Block (HRB)

NetApp (NTAP)

British Petroleum (BP)

AT&T (T)

Wells Fargo Bank (WFC)

Enterprise Products (EPD)

Foot Locker (FL)

Bank of Nova Scotia (BNS)

Iron Mountain (IRM)

AES (AES)

Flowers Foods   FLO

Fluor    FLR

Oneok   OKE

## Conclusion:

Now that you have a little guidance, some direction, some additional knowledge and some suggestions, get out there and buy some stocks. There was a Chinese proverb that I read once that said...

"The journey of a thousand miles begins with one step."

I know it might seem a little scary and intimidating at first, but you can do it. And once you do it, I bet you will find it just as addicting as I do.

I think it was Terry Pratchett that said...

"The worst thing you can do is nothing."

Buckle down and just make it happen. You will make some mistakes along the way, but don't worry about it. Just keep at it and when you hit those ten- and twenty-year marks and you realize all those ains, you will be so happy that you did. As a matter of fact, you will probably look back and say, why didn't I do it sooner?

You can find additional books by the author online at...

Amazon.com

Goodreads.com

curiouskelley.com

These books have to have at least 100 pages for the spine thickness to be correct. The following pages are just to burn up space to make the 100 pages –

Notes:
_____
_____

_____
_____

**Notes:**
_____
_____
_____
_____

**Notes:**
_____
_____

_____
_____

**Notes:**
_____
_____

_____
_____

**Notes:**
_____
_____

_____
_____

**Notes:**
_____
_____

_____
_____

**Notes:**
_____
_____

_____
_____

**Notes:**
_____
_____

_____
_____

**Notes:**
_____
_____

_____
_____

**Notes:**
_____
_____

_____
_____

**Notes:**
_____
_____

_____
_____

**Notes:**
_____
_____


_____
_____

**Notes:**
_____
_____

_____
_____

**Notes:**
_____
_____

_____
_____

**Notes:**
_____
_____

_____
_____

**Notes:**
_____
_____

_____
_____

**Notes:**
_____
_____

_____
_____

**Notes:**
_____
_____

_____
_____

**Notes:**
_____
_____

_____
_____

**Notes:**
_____
_____

_____

_____

**Notes:**
_____
_____

_____
_____

**Notes:**
_____
_____

_____
_____

**Notes:**
_____
_____

_____
_____

**Notes:**
_____
_____

_____
_____

**Notes:**
___
___
___
___

**Notes:**
_____
_____

_____

_____

**Notes:**
_____
_____

_____

_____

**Notes:**
_____
_____
_____
_____

**Notes:**
_____
_____
_____
_____

**Notes:**
_____
_____

_____
_____

**Notes:**

**Notes:**
_____
_____

_____
_____

**Notes:**
_____
_____

_____

_____

**Notes:**

**Notes:**
_____
_____

_____
_____

**Notes:**
_____
_____

_____
_____

**Notes:**
_____
_____


_____
_____

**Notes:**
_____
_____
_____
_____

**Notes:**
_____
_____

_____
_____

**Notes:**
_____
_____

_____
_____

**Notes:**
_____
_____

_____
_____

**Notes:**
_____
_____

_____
_____

**Notes:**
_____
_____

_____
_____

**Notes:**
_____
_____

_____
_____

**Notes:**
_____
_____

_____
_____